MindScape Excavation

Caroline Gay Way

ISBN: 978-0-244-69099-1

Contents

Pandora

They call to me — the voices — from their dark
cajoling — persuading
screaming sometimes
sometimes in rage
there is a childlike voice
that sings — In foreign tongue
and I
feel wistful for the dark of earth
the coolness of the under moss

Like prayer — mist rises
toward the alchemy of gold
as sun is pulled to earth
and trees reach up for darkness
slowly — as it gathers round the stars

It is intense for me — intense
to be left — so long with voices
                                        drowning
as night sounds of the earth
                                        release
the dark scent of cicadas
                                          keeps me sane
                                                      and yet
and yet I am worn down
as I am quite alone — one of a kind
the gods did leave us long ago

All other creatures roam
the wide world's freedoms flow
like birds — I long to see them fly
free from confines of the box

they are only voices after all
to keep them captive is a crime
perhaps — perhaps

an open heart is better than one closed
an open box is better than
the shadow that it throws

£2
£2
£3.25
£2
£2
£2
£2
£2
£2.70
£2
£3

Shop Till You Drop

The Manufacturers Dream Amalgamation

Please — drift with your trolleys
and do take your pick
grab multiple packets
spend more — that's the trick!

Swallow our pills to cure your ills
your health's in our tablets
our bottles and creams
we provide answers to your shopping dreams
so you can continue in optimum health
and keep on providing our fabulous wealth

The things that we sell can make people unwell
but then we can fix it and tricks it and mix it

The things that we sell can make people too fat
then we can trim them and slim them and gym
them

Your health's in our tablets
our bottles and creams
we want you to continue
your bright shopping dreams

As you drift with our baskets
oh please take your pick
get that great bargain
you'll have to be quick

it's all brightly wrapped
so each pack's a present
to pick from the aisle
is so easy and pleasant

Now don't you bother to chop or to dice
it's all in the packet so yummy and nice
with cellophane wrapping its cooked in a trice
with no washing up
you don't have to think twice
it's all done in plastic and polly-styrene
your kitchens all shrink-wrapped
hygienically clean

Just cook in your programmed imagination
Oliver/Blumenthal cook for the nation

We have the readies all perfectly wrapped
we keep in the goodness so perfectly trapped
you have the readies to perfectly buy
its perfect – delicious — so why don't you try

Luckily you're sugar programmed
Luckily to like our products
Luckily we have your buying patterns
        right here on file –so smile
Luckily we get to know just what you want
Luckily before you do
Luckily we'll suggest it
Luckily we're your friend
Luckily you can friend us on Facebook

Luckily we can see
    if you are swimming with us
    in the cyberspace sea
Luckily your movements are known to us
    no fuss
Luckily we can share everything
Luckily we only want to make
    your buying experience an event
    until you're spent

Health's all in a bottle a tube or a pill
the things that we sell here?
they won't make you ill
you can be sure that there's no trick
to finding a cure just for you — if your sick

So if through stress
your health is less
we have the answers here — under one roof
just look at our magazines if you want proof
you don't have to worry
our foods carbon dated
and bar-code sedated

As good shepherds we herd them
in loyalty fields
and look very carefully
at their buying yields
branded we fold them
behind coded baa-rs
we think of them fondly
as being ours

Their movements are watched now
and deftly encoded
no freedoms eroded
info-tell uploaded

Now the drive to be thin is making them fatter
the fashions not thinking but endlessly chatter
now sitting in silence in real time with friends
while facebooking others
while twittering trends
while endlessly tapping the button that sends
while tracking the trackless in deep cyber space
while programs are running to keep up the pace
Now physically dormant they get supersize
The sofas their playground
and doughnuts the prize

Our medical gold mine will give you a fix
do have some more of our new sweet food mix
and now that you're thirsty
buy some fizz pop
one hundred varieties
just in this one shop

You're feeling puffy
oh that's such a shame
but really there's no one else that's to blame

We'll welcome your waddle
through our hospital door
we'll put you right
you can be sure

Our up-market hospital's clean and bright
whatever is wrong we'll put you right
we've thousands of pills to get you well
so we can enable your basket to swell

It's the junk food to slim pills inviting swing door
buy crisps
need our potions
oh do try some more
we'll be all the choices
that you'll ever make
and provide you the dream
from which you'll never wake

We really just want you
to be there to spend
we want you to shop
till you drop in the end

The House

No Hansel no — someone might see

There's no-one here
we've been right round
just smell that gingerbread
we're hungry — we're lost
what harm can it do?
no-one will ever know.

Well, we'll just take a little bit then
just off the windowsill here

And that was the start of it
she was angry with us —
we'd eaten the whole window sill
fallen asleep as the shadows lengthened
we almost ran when she caught us
I burst into tears an' she took pity

I'm so sorry — I said with tears in my eyes
Hansel said nothing

We've been wandering for days.
we've been sleeping in dark hollows
sleeping in forest fear

Hansel makes his stories
bigger somehow

We don't like our fathers new wife
we think our father is bewitched
he met her in the tavern
since mother died he's been 'in cups'
maybe that's how come he walked off
left us all alone
he drank an' didn't remember
thirsty work chopping — he'd say
he always told us
he was drinking to forget

He earned little from chopping wood
after mother died his earnings went for drink
he'd bring us bread when he remembered
bread — I'd call after him when he went off
breadcrumbs — he'd call back as he trudged away
most times he'd forget

When she'd heard our story
she took us in
gave us a proper feast
with milk and bread and cheese
her cottage had a cheery hearth
her kitchen warm and cosy
as the evening grew colder
shadows formed around the house

Well, my dears, that's quite a tale to be sure
they call me Mrs Ginger round these parts
you can stay with me and help me if you like

Mrs Ginger made sweets and gingerbread
for shops in towns and villages
all along the river
her little house smelt wonderful every day
full of jars of toffee
and beautiful coloured sweets
liquorice and lollypops hung from the rafters
she taught us how to make them all
she was kind to us both
we began to forget our life before

Hansel started going off to town
telling tales
in ale houses for drinks
she tried to lock him in sometimes
'cos he was too young for drinking
Hansel was well angry
one winter's day they argued
Mrs Ginger's skirt caught fire
the sugar in the fabric flared
into her beautiful long hair
I ran fast to get up water
we couldn't save her
burnt to a crisp she was
she'd gone so quick
I cried myself to sleep that night

All those years I've wondered
why father had left us
Hansel was in his cups one night
I asked him why father had left us
he started laughing

What is it Hansel — I said
it's not funny
I miss our father sorely

Do you Gretel — he said
I couldn't wait to get away
I took us off where he couldn't find us
so we could have an adventure
to make our fortune
that's what we did Gretel
found this place and made our fortune
shadows lengthened as he told it

The shops and bakers sell
our gingerbread and our ginger snaps
she had a small ginger plantation
behind the house
Hansel's ginger wine is famous now
and very strong
Hansel has sold our story
to go in a book

Hansel calls her a witch now
when he is telling his tales

Truth is she was very kind to us
so I never will

SweetBox 2020

The queue always started
before eight o'clock –
as everyone in the line
was rather large
the line lengthened
very quickly
by nine – when the shutters opened
it stretched around the corner

SweetBox outlets are now as prolific
as the well known fast food chains
that fetter the world's great cities
with its fritters and fries

In Roman times
there were bread and circuses
to keep people happy
in 2020 it is burgers
baseball and SweetBox.

As the SweetBox doors open
people shuffle into long familiar lines
in front of the sugar sweet confectioners
they all need the fix
that sweetens their day
small eyes in fleshy faces
avidly scan the brightly coloured boards
for their daily SweetBox deal

Day glow coloured boxes

already filled with sweet deals
are stacked in trays
behind the pink uniforms
of the sugar smelling
sweetly smiling short skirt servers

How can I help you today
is the carefully crafted question
they ask with a bright coached smile

You have a sweet day now
each one says
as each of the large clientele
are happily handed
their hugely generous
GoodyBox.

A steady stream of cars
begin gliding heavily
into the drive-thru
collecting pre orders
with bucket sized reward cups
of fizzy pop for all the family

In the trucker park
pretty pink Sweeties
bring cell phoned pre-orders
out to sedentary truckers

The highly successful slogan
Can do Candy — Door to Door
environmentally friendly
delivery vans drive
slowly round city streets
stimulating sweet thoughts
to reward stressed wage slave days

Stop me and buy some — Sugar
is the name of the game
used streetwise
in flirtatious innuendo

Sometimes people notice
how large they are getting
and buy magazines
full of expensive ways
of getting rid of excess
surgeons grow immensely wealthy
taking out or redistributing fat
depending on client preference

If anyone runs out of candy
there is a drug store on every street corner
open till midnight

As one rather slim politician
was heard to say in private
It's the sweetest way to cull
an over large population
After all — he chuckled —
life on the street is short and sweet

The Voigle

The story of the Voigle
is a very sorry tale
because at first the Voigle would
just cry and sigh and wail

Hill villagers came over
to see what was amiss
but all the Voigle then would do
was scream and boo and hiss

And people came from miles around
to stop the dreadful noise
but sadly went back home again
far wiser girls and boys

The Voigle was a sorry sight
its tears rolled down its chin
they shook their heads and plugged their ears
from Voigle's dreadful din

And packed their bags
and went away to find a quieter hill
the doctor came and gave the Voig
a nasty bitter pill

And pull your self together said
in grave and boorish tone
and went away and left the Voigle
damp and quite alone

And — oh my eyes are quite wrung out
the Voigle said one day
the sun is shining in the sky
so let us all make hay

But there was no one on the hill
to hear its happy cry
so off into the sunset flew
the Voigle by and by

And no one heard the Voigle more
though rumours flew around
and there were cries when Voigle feathers
fluttered to the ground

The Voigle's dead we can come back
the people laugh and cheer
as high above the Voigle gulped
and shed a lonely tear

And in its throat the lump was hard
it flew on in the rain
I just came back to play with you
it never spoke again

In wind and rain the Voigle flies
you've heard its cries and moans
forever flying damply on
a bag of hungry bones

And if you think to look for it
you'll see it in the rain
just look up high and you will see
its thin and weary frame

We didn't mean it Voigle
you could shout into the sky
and if your kind you'll throw to it
a freshly made mud pie

The Locust Eaters

Alien letter home

They seem to have to take everything
off the land and wrap it
in bright colours
it is wrapped
by others who they do not know

Those who pick are not the same
as those who are the mixers and the changers
of the grown abundance
the mixers sell changed food with date stamps
people think makes stuff so safe and sealed

The people locust on bright packets
in the bright food temples
suckling slick tongued
on some colour bubbled slurp
made safe and clean
by those who make and mix

The people do not know it's eating from land
when it is wrapped
boxed it's safe and sugar fatted good

Their word 'soil' is their word for dirt
to make a clean thing dirty is to soil it
they call their soil 'dirt'
they do not want to know things grow in dirt
earth also is their word for dirt and soil

Once — before they swarmed
their air was clean
before their infestation
no dirt was ever in or on the earth
waters washed pristine
the shores of lake and stream

In this age the water ways are chocked
with rotting wrappers — plastic bags
wrap their land in all that's torn and tattered
covering the man made mixes

Everything that's taken from the land's
bright colour wrapped
neon 'buy us' wares shout to them
all along their halls of plenty

Natural is old fashioned now
except in filmic safety
be wary of the dangerously real
beware of dirty earth

Buy man-you-fractured goods

Buy the disconnection
from the earth's abundance

Buy chemical enhanced concoctions

Buy into extra sweetness
extra salt fuelled flavours

As Locust Eaters swarm

Buy — bye

The Square Tree

And God Was Made Man

In the beginning Man said
let there be stars
and he got out his ruler
and squared them off
into nice neat lines
into exact uniformly shining cubes
spaced in perfect symmetry
around the squared trajectory grid
of perfect night sky

On the second day
Man created heaven and earth
in heaven there were fast cars
beer and everything else that man liked
on earth he caused grass to grow short
in perfect lines

Man caused trees to grow straight trunked
with foliage that grew cube shaped
that's a neat job he said
as he looked at his handiwork
Man made animals and birds
to hunt and kill for food
and an abundant sea with fish to net
he caused fish that grew in rectangles
so they could fit straight
into bright coloured packets

you can guess the easy to cut shapes
Man's animals and birds were in

Man made concrete to flow over all the earth
much tidier
he said smiling
then man made woman
you can imagine what she looked like
she was top heavy
and perfectly compliant
I've done a good job
said man

Vincent's Last Day

Something is attracting crows
more than usual he thought
as he unwrapped his brushes

His shouts disturbed them
from time to time
a self appointed scarecrow

This would be a painting of their gathering flight
he knew they would descend again
towards their unseen carrion feast

First the angry curses then the gun
his ragged ear ringing with sound
dimming the crows rasping cries
until more gentle sound returned
to rest upon the field

Oil brushed canvas as he worked fast
to capture the energy that surrounded him
into slowly hardening colour
that would hold the moment in time and colour
when crows flew up disturbed
as he ran along the disappearing road
into the corn and lobbed a stone

Suddenly the world turned on it's heel
in sunhat shaded eyes he stared
speculatively into middle distance

pulsing heat shimmered
gently disturbing afternoon air
sun heavy corn heads bowed
in time stilled glare
below crows raucous cacophony

Was that not exactly where he'd sat
the day before — further down the track
painting the bright energy feast
of sun spilled woven corn

was not this just how the scene would be
if he were lying there alone in death

The paradox — a painting
rich in life and hidden death
beneath the corn and crows

Theo could sell such a picture
a picture of an artists death
in the landscape
a picture of an artists death
in the landscape he had just painted
a painting of gun shot startled crows
gathering around
the hidden hardening body
in middle distance below a churning carrion sky

Vincent smiled this would be a harvest
not only for the grim reaper
but harvest for Theo
live artists do not sell well

this would set the matter straight
this final golden cornfield gift
he took a final swig
and wiped away a drop of wine
he was finished
his painting was finished
soon the crows would find him

The Pulse of an Ocean

Strong shafts of sunlight
stretching down
reach deep into the waters dark
illuminating treasures lost
        beneath percussive waves

Sand sifts
        the salt swilled lift
as brine brimmed life within solution
                                        stirs
while currents riff
        pulsating drifts of seaweed strands
                        with unseen strumming
shadows dapple under sea

A grand piano drifting slowly down
                        on oceans back
                enfolding octaves into depths

A woman's body
                lost to air
is very slowly sinking
                as long hair unwinds
                    extends around her
ringed hands spread
        with arms extended
                        playing a silent fugue

High above her sinking form
            gold rides on dancing waves in sunlight
burns on ancient sea surf face
                              no trace
                              is left of storm's
tempestuous rage
                              no sounds of timbers
breaking
a lone gull cries

exploring waves reach out toward the land
foam frilled palms stroke smooth the sand
                              a fingersmith for amber
                        precious stones and
sometimes gold

Tide rising in moon fuelled motion
                                 turns over driftwood
examines what to take
                               unto itself
and what to leave behind in air

Sea is warm sometimes as blood
             and lies still languid in lagoons
or is as stone with ice packed cold
of splintered heart
        is quiet after storm

Sea reaches yearning ruffled waves
towards its sea spawned progeny
the water walkers pumping salt laced blood
will drift along the shore in summer
or under winters cloud
will quietly absorb the pulse of waves

The Birds — The Birds

The Seagull pack of peck hard beaks
lift as one from cold grey waves
to turn to slope
their surfed air glide
toward the inland
roof shine hills

Across cold marshlands
trees stand tall in ice hard fields
sentinel on naked wintered branches
at sunset
a murder of crows
form a silent still silhouette
watching — waiting
malign against a blood red sky

Crow's beak is turned as one
towards the on shore wind
an heraldic regiment
gathering dark
in winter trees

The town is small below crows' wheeling flocks
fat-wrapped people make warm roofs
but leave few scraps

Indictment

Man has changed to less the eating from the sea

changed to less — the taste of eating from the land

both Man and Crow have known this place

Crow has known this place before man came

Man leaves flat bloodied offerings
on his roads
for Crow to glean

but it is not enough
no It is not enough

they are fat wrapped enough
for us to eat our fill
and so
and now
Crow will

With guttural cry the beaks descend
as arms are raised in shocked defence
windows shatter — beaks attack
could this beginning — be the end

Christina Rossetti's Southwold Christmas

In that bleak midwinter
frosty wind made moaning sounds
around the corners of his Suffolk house
we'd come with William
our dear friend Morris
for Christmas

One sparkling winters morning
I had cause to know the hardness of the frosted earth –
as I slipped and felt the stone cold ice
quite bruised - I had to return to the house

Snow kept falling
snow on snow
as I stepped carefully treading in Williams footprints
through the ringing snow flecked air
towards the angel church
that Christmas morning long ago

We stood before the crib
as if we were visiting kings
dressed in our velvet fur trimmed robes
leaving our little gifts for the poor
in an eternal moment
I was there with the Christ child
feeling the immensity
of the presence before me

High in the church rafters
the roof angels gathered
and gazed down
as our voices swell towards them
my heart sang with the joy of it

As we returned the snow began to fall again
musing I watched in candle light
took up a quill - began to write
with angel feather long into the night

Broken Bone China

Picking through the broken bits

I mused on snatches
of their life I knew

We met at a party
just off sunset strip
we married quite soon
we were very happy
all our time together

The white wine we shared on summer evenings
the books he was writing
a play that was quite successful
his work with damaged children
a warm smile

I pause looking at long lost patterns
seeing form that once was
now just bright fragments
that once had use
drew eyes
his warm smile
    lingering in memory
        now is gone
            from this place
both of them are gone

One be-boned is heir to the cosmic drift of stars
one has drifted south
too sad to think and too bereft

Without them I pick through the broken china
that was once part of lives
I know the feel of treasured moments
amongst the brokenness of bones

Dora's Patina

In memory of the sculptress Dora Gordine

Process
touching surface – building
from the deeps of clay
deeply felt — distilling soft flesh
her strong sculptors' hands
work clay and stone
draw stilled life from living form
in dance or contemplation

Patinas
building layers — into form
ultimately the alchemy
of liquid metals' fire
confirms a moment
caught in time

So now as years progress
worked into galleries
the forms gaze back at those who pass
those who stare and talk in hallowed tones
and those not passing
in silent galleried shadows
reflecting moonlight
the still of formed sculpture
the distillation
of the makers art
accumulates a patina of dust

Patina
a different place
sculptures hard held living moment
stands
out in elements

In slow time corrosion forms on form
surfacing surface
developing
through storms
swirling the patina
of earth's rotation into days
of sun and wind and rain
the lick of lichen
slowly spreads

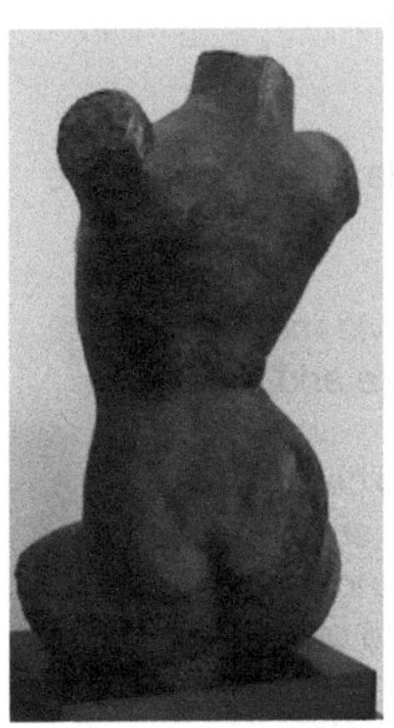

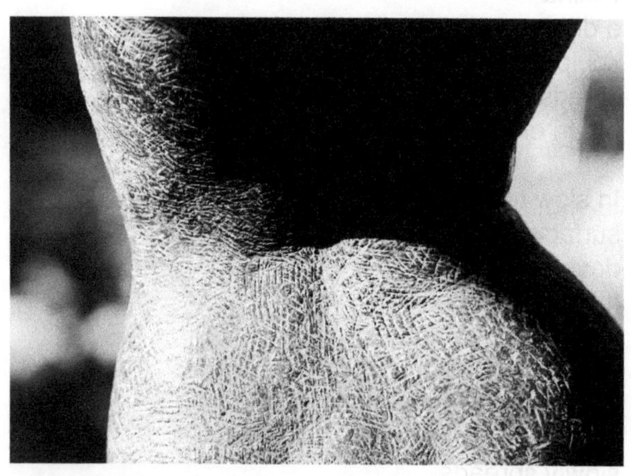

Patina of Dora
in her life
in her studio
she layers — layers — of surface
of mind
of process
of love-lived vivid moments
fragments of life and memories

A patina of choices
of countries — smart vibrant cities
many friends and faces
the avant-guard of a Paris
overflown with flapper girls
in tight cloche hats
dark vamps flirt with long cigarettes

as the outrageous cacophony of jazz
spills out onto somersaulting streets
Paris — nineteen twenty five
exciting times to be alive
Josephine Baker's Dance
is all the rage — swirling sensation of the age
as is Black Bottom — from Club Cotton
eyes widen as monocles are press to eyes
in mock surprise

Dora also a rising star — her art discovered
both ladies vibrant young exotic
with reputations glasses raised
the long string click of beads
and heels on Paris pavements
making mercurial mischief
laughing in late night Paris lamplight
both intwined in Paris swirl — kiss curl
and did Jo's feet in syncopated time
still her body for the Gordine muse
to take the shape of laughing buttocks
deft finger-smith from flesh to stone peruse

On to London circles dance apace
as swirling cocktails mix with laughter's flow
as streams of new configured thought
and witty talk with late night candles glow

Dora becomes a bride to English aristocracy
together they shelter hidden desires
from the world's gaze
she does not starve in a garret
but builds a layered house
from the intriguing gold ringed bargain
of convenience and company
she builds a layered life

Her life explores the far flung places
of features - those of different races
of work defining life and self
her plaster sculptures gather now upon a shelf
the tall room gathers light around
the sculptured now on plinths have places found

Her sculptors skill
combined with that of wife
her forms endure still
within them still is life

Chopping Board Tales

From the beginning
it witnessed my first attempts
at married life
my first attempts at cooking

I had never been a kitchen girl
my shoes were too exotic

But here I was expected to keep us fed

I had only shopped before
for fashion with
a daddy size allowance

Now I looked into poverties dull eyes
and stared back at her
the chopping board witness to my drudgery

Taken to another place
the chopping board absorbed the threats to life
absorbed the drunken violence

And yet in kitchen sunshine
little fingers reaching up
searched its surface
for sticky rewards of bread and jam
while its wooden surface felt
the heat of dropping tears

Gretel

Walking by the sea she hears no waves
the iPod keeps her bubbled mood enhanced
synthetic sound digitally cleansed
pulsates
entwining her pulsating blood
her frequency is not trouble by gulls
small stones beneath her feet
do not disturb her
stride
in sweat shop
shock absorbent shoes
made half a world away

the streets are empty now
as cyberspace engulfs and swallows souls

play inside my children - play inside
it is safer so much safer- deep inside
the cushioned and imagined worlds
of sugared dreams
as The Real recedes
becomes unsafe
and so we guard our children's lives
keep them cocooned and close and watched
as we too
in turn
are watch bewitched

few children now roam free
of digital connection

In our world Hansel leaves a trail of crisps
behind his bars he's fattened up
with double choc-o-lated doughnuts
Pops pizza burgers topped with chips
into his imprisoned mouth

Gretel now she's free
is walking by the sea
she hears no waves

My Deep World Maps

I crawled in time
across my deep world maps
I look now on
the furled curled parchments
of my time and place
where they are stacked
in far off rooms   and some
I think are lost
the old rolled maps
in random stacks
some sealed with wax
now gather dust

Sometimes in flick'ring candle light
I study long
 at routes I took
and those not taken
tracking into sand
a tear will fall at times for both
and blur the faded coloured ink

So still
my time here slows
I do not feel the spinning earth
as if inertia holds my pace
through time and rushing winds of space

The Map of Now is fathoms deep
it shows the way through trackless wastes
of time of mountains
that I want to climb
and seas to cross
where treasures have been found and lost
some hidden in the wrecks that sunk
wherein my merchant's fortune mostly drowned

In time it takes to blink an eye
and live a life
there are now countless parchments rolled
to be discovered or be thrown away
returned to dust

Yet I crawl on
beneath the sun and stars
that light my way
of time in space
as new maps seeming blank
roll out before my now
they will be filled
I know not how

The Flower

The flower you hold in the palm of your hand
has travelled through eons
through the furnace of stars
though trackless wastes in time
journeying the aching cold
the vast dark distances
of space — of space
through earth's tempestuous pregnancy
to midwife life from molten rock
through ravages of storm and searing heat
so to evolve into the mist of that first dawn
the first dawn
in which a flower ever bloomed
as earth drew breath
and saw the first unfolding petals
open to the sky
a fragile offering of scent perfumed the air
a blush of colour in the breeze
a shy lover coming out into a waiting world
the lover's gift
this bloom you cradle now
holds all this precious essence
a potent heady alchemy
of time and space
through which it flowed
through which it flowers
into this moment
into your hand

Not Broken

Kintsugi — to repair with gold; The art of repairing ceramics with gold or silver lacquer and understanding that the piece is more beautiful for having been broken.

The world breaks everyone then some become strong at the broken places — Hemingway

In my little girl arms
my being bowl brim full of trust and love
is carried with care for all to see
its brand new effervescent mixture fizzes brightly
my eyes and shoes shine
with 6 year old exuberance
A first dark encounter with the wider world
shatters moments of my being

into shards with contents spilled
and I no longer know how it was made
spun with sunlit smiles
fires burned in its fragile alchemy
I felt it was so strong
so indestructible
as now I see
with over spilling eyes
its broken vulnerability
in that moment
I wished for the earth to swallow me up
slowly – painfully
I return to clay
painfully my child hands begin to coil a new pot
dried hardened and adorned with bright colours
my heart again swells to see it shine
and yet somewhere in hidden corners
I keep the broken pieces of the first
gradually dust wrapped
I reached out for them carefully
one jagged piece at a time
in life I learnt the art of kintsugi
though some shards are as yet unfound
the golden mending warms the heart and eye
my early being bowl is now reformed
and I am carrying again some vital essence
in the most beautiful bowl in my possession
carried aloft for all to see
the golden crack filled network
that is the mending of the broken me

Peregrine Fellows

Peregrine Fellows always had on the same
I wore it when I met Ted Hughes hat
he always sat in the same chair
I always get there ahead of the rush
under the corner light
at the Isambard Kingdom public house
at the unfashionable end of Kings Rd

Young people entered the Kingdom pub
with a sense of wonder
that it hadn't been pine table eatery changed
since the swinging sixties

It was unbelievably swinging
Peregrine would answer
with a twinkle in his eye
if anyone asked

'I happen to have a sixties poem with me
would you like to hear it – mine's a pint'
he would take off the large elastic band
and rifle throughout his
bit dog-eared like me note book

Peregrine was the reason the pub had survived
his people had money
was the lucky tosser goss'
'my people are all gone
I am the last of the line'
he would say with mock moroseness
as he toasted the muse
privately his set thought he was lucky
to get Aubrey to publish Slim Volume
conversely his readings were well attended
by the Chelsea Arts Club crowd

His flat around the corner
'I've been there since the ark'
came with the pub
only Peregrine knew it was there
everyone else had forgotten
where the door in the wall led to
even Scroggins' grandson
who now ran the pub
had forgotten the flat

'We humour the old codger
the cost-an-arm-an-a-leg lawyers
said we couldn't change a thing
in the Isambard Kingdom
without that damn old lush's consent'
anyway Scroggins was shrug shoulders lazy

Peregrine's faded pub chair
was surrounded by elegant '50s framed photos
'old and dear friends actually
we partied all night on the Kings Road
had breakfast at Picasso's'

'That's an interesting picture'

Peregrine was jerked out of his
'I can see them all clear as day' reverie

the young man pointed to a snap of Peregrine
complete with hat in the club photo
Marilyn with her 'smile could light up the room'
and Arthur Miller and the AC/DC boy
having the one up there with the boy
in public view he knew was rather risky
but he so loved the memory of that night
dancing wildly with Marilyn and the boy

He gave the young man a overly bright
'I thought I'd got away with it' smile
'yes dear boy Marilyn's smile is hard to miss
I sewed her into her dress that night you know'

'so you're quite handy with a needle and thread
— may I?'
The young man pulled up an adjacent chair

'of course dear boy'
enthusiasm in the charm of his voice
but not in his heart or smile
Peregrine thought
of how he had sewn up the sack
and noticed his hands were shaking a little
this modern young man
looked so similar to the boy
he looks like a young Greek god in the photo

'He was my uncle'

'Who?'

'Uncle Jack — in the photo with Marilyn'

'I never knew his real name'

'we did some digging recently'

Peregrine looked alarmed

'digging where?'
steady — steady keep calm — don't give
anything away

'family archives — trying to find out what
happened to him'

'I haven't a clue — not a clue
he just disappeared'
I was heartbroken

‘So you've no idea where he went’

Peregrine took a swig of his beer
not to Heaven certainly
it was so long ago
more years than I care to remember
who could forget his sleek young torso
Alan Turing was there that night
we were all great friends
the boy took quite a shine to Alan
I remember — quite a shine
had rather a row about it actually
I never saw him again
he said such vile and hurtful things that night
Peregrin fingered the silver top of his ebony
sword stick
I was incandescent — there was so much blood

‘Gran will be pleased I tracked you down’

‘I never knew he had family
never spoke about his past only his future’

‘we’d like a copy of that photo
if you didn’t mind — for our family archives’

‘Yes yes come again
I’ll have one ready for you
come in next week — do’

Peregrine frowned as uncharacteristically early
he got up to go
back at his high ceilinged flat
he lit the fire
ye gods it can be cold in June
he went to the bureau
and brought out a drawer full of their photos
the one with the boy naked
wearing the old feather hat at a rakish angle
produced a tear of self pity
the lines of their naked young bodies
were so very beautiful
but what if there were questions
long ago crimes were coming to light these days
was there still DNA on his silver topped cane

Slowly Peregrine Fellows ignited
his colourful past
to the flames of a funeral pyre
he never left his flat again

Rip – Rip – R.I.P

Psycho

Caught in a sudden flurry of
slowly floating feathers snow
she thought she would be *cosy fire* home
before it got really bad

Minutes later going down the slipway
onto the motorway
she realised it was
really snowing in *windscreen-wiper* earnest

She gripped the *white knuckle* steering wheel
tighter and tighter
peering blindly joining the
I'm running out of road here people inside lane

Blinding monster lorries
lit up *cotton fluff* flurries of dense snow
packed on the motorway treadmill
she could see *white night* nothing

Headlights on full
only lit the white floating wall
to a mesmerising brightness
within in a terrifying
where the hell's the next exit half hour

Lorries tailgated
her *I'm going as fast as I can* crawl
her tiny metal car
was her *I can't see a thing*
island of fear.

Looming through the fear and darkness
there was a sign
to a *place I've never heard of*
motorway exit

A long twisted journey
loomed an out of the darkness pub
with *stay here if you are really desperate* cabins

The man behind the bar
had a beery *I'm completely sober* smile
it was his *I'm desperate for sex*
but I'm not going to show it
eyes that bothered her most.

But she put on her best
I'm not going to notice anything weird
be polite but not encouraging smile
as she asked for a room

But her eyes strayed beyond him
towards the over bright eyes
of the under glass animals
in freeze frame action behind his desk

As he showed her over to the completely grotty
but I'll have to make the best of it cabin
she hoped they were not alone
as she knew she was completely
off the beaten track and it was quiet
too snow surrounded quiet

The water in the *stray pubic hair* shower
was piping hot
pulling the *seen better days* shower curtain
she saw a little bar of *it's been used before* soap

Returning to the empty bar
he slowly finished his drink
checked in on his mother
she was sitting stone still
in the *she's been there for years* rocking chair

He hated *I pretend I don't but I do* females
he could hear the cabin woman
using up all the *it costs a fortune* hot water
'probably she will have the heating on
all night because of the snow
in her cosy *forgot to change the sheets* cabin'

The shower was going on and onto her naked
I mustn't think about that body
he bent over as if in pain slapping his hands
over his *why not mother?* ears

He took a large knife
out of the *I must stop her* drawer
he opened her *mother won't like this* cabin door

Quietly he moved across
the *shut up mother* room
slowly sliding open the
I shouldn't be here door

He could see her
through the shower curtain
'mother chose that shower curtain
I never liked that
stab it tear it pattern'

Never never never
stab scream stab
now she's just how I like them — quiet

His taxidermist eye already saw
I can do a good job on her possibilities

The Emperor's New Poet

In wakeful moments
I eat blue chips
on midnight shells
spiked gall in hand
oiling the screaming dark aroma
of skeletal dances
I endlessly scratch
swan sheets
vainly edged in bloods dark gold
fears separate souls
from light's long taper

He lies in sweating moss
a multitude of distilled times
grate his pallor
pulling twisted wire debris
he stands a swaying garland
as starlings echo
in the roar of falling sun

Poison steeps elegance to the few
who can escape
the quills of ravens
or crows straight flight
sufficient in the darkening drifts of sky
cry lament as days edge crumples

The iron stab — does nothing

Clearing weaves of tangled stems
their wheeling once engendered life
now stalking time are winter broken
towards the Lebanon hills

In the howl of red rimmed night
expectant white moths
write on night air
and I will ply my nets
in star sea currents
the jasmine will not bloom till spring

The Gulls

With acknowledgements to Daphne Du Maurier's short story The Birds and the Alfred Hitchcock film.

This poem was first preformed at Crystal Waters Australia in 2002 and was inspired by an actual experience at Surfers Paradise

Writers sometimes see the future
Daphne du Maurier certainly did
she lived in Cornwall
and had experienced
the eyes of gulls
their bullying and determined ways
their propensity to cluster
around the munching tourist trade
how they scrapped over scraps
she saw levels of demented concentration
focus that bordered on addiction

Slavering dogs in a medieval court
do not match them
these winged pack hunters
are clannish and cold
fierce as the salt whipped winds from the Arctic

Soft fat fleshed and TV blanched
the vacuous visitors filled faces
and fattened rounded stomachs
to pocket pulling proportions

Gulls wing watched
the weaving sun baked Saturday streets
a star spangled summer celebration
through holiday heat waving crowds
in pulsating U.S. style parade
Mac D's had come to town

On the 5th of July in Falmouth
something snapped
the fire cracking fourth of July fireworks
had disturbed their evening
seagulls wheeled and whirled
over the salt licked town
swearing and screeching harshly to each other
throughout the night
like disgruntled fishwives
they cursed on the wing
swirling through the darkness
like angry angels

As above so below
foul mouthed Falmouthians
tossed in their beds and made plans to cull

Full-bodied tourists sweated
bulging burgered bulk in squeaking beds
kids kicked at cot bars
sulkily screaming
for pop — for crisps -- to play Nintendo
teens and twenty somethings
turned on and tuned out
as the starlit sky was churned
by the wheeling fractal frenzy
of sea-gulled shadows
swirling disturbing

At high-noon the local Concrite twins
next fix needy
emerged predatorily from the Crow's Nest
perched high above the town
sun glassed gummed and identically ipodded
the twins swaggered slowly seaward
the hated glare penetrating spiked skulls
bedevilled brains and opportunity were soon
lightly fingering their sweating empty pockets

One looked over
one looked out
cold eyes casing
the open door an invitation
the bag on the table - open
the over ripe purse – ready for plucking

the hard hand pinch-pecked
and pocket swallowed

Fast footsteps flew and drew
twisted harbour alleys into shadowed safety
entrails spilled
cards – coins – crumpled notes

The predatory pair picked over contents
the dry fish stink merged with sweat
and something more enticing
something more mouth watering
was nudging their twin Concrite nostrils
an arresting aroma
came curvaceously curling
into Concrite consciousness

MacDominAnt burgers and fries

Crouching bodies straightened mesmerised
the twins turned towards town
urgent in their need for the fast food fix
of MacD's delicious delights
craving caught and cussed
oily with sun sweated skin
and ripening red necked pimples
drawn like two magnetised pins
like dogs – they followed the scent

MacDominAnt's smiling demon ant logo
beckoned with bright red plasticity
with smell of deeply dreamed
hypnotically honed
fiendish flavours of fantasy fries
mingling erotically with big bunned burgers

Devilicious!

MacDominAnt's ant horns
visually echoed it's demon ant smile
each bag topped with a long fry
curved in the smile/horn shape
children ate the smile or
devil horn depending on mood

it was a benediction of sorts
a ritual eating of flesh and fries
and red ant effervescent blood
little devils sick of sin
slurping sticky red slush
from round rimmed cups
the thin red smile stain extended logoed lips

Smile stamped and smugly
they sauntered fat bagged and harbour-wards
in Sunday step towards the gulls
bits of buns and burgers
were greedily gobbled

Gaunt gimlet gull-eyes wing watched
twixt earth and heaven

they did not fall as angels sometimes do
one wing folded
diving so suddenly
so deeply at the prey
others followed fiercely
disturbing the sea-slapped air
disturbing pensioners at prayer
with irreverent clownish squawking
self-served with swerving swoop

Screaming screaming screaming

Gulls took the burger bread
Take eat — this is my Body
gull spilled the effervescent blood
they took the cup
worshipping the craving image
the red ant Christ

They came in droves
breathless little children
stuff suffer stuff
puff puffer puff
little children getting larger
getting more of what they wanted
getting the fast food fix
so were the gulls

Addiction is careless of consequence
so are gulls

At first a fat fleshed fingered fist

fought for custody of a half torn bag of fries
and smiling devil's horn
but torn fleshed iron smell of blood
stimulated further feasting and flocking
stirring sky
fathers fought feathered gull addicts
strong single fathers — out for the day
suddenly doing what fathers should
fighting for family
protecting progeny
mothers swarmed into shops
dragging bedraggled screamers
until the glass shattered

Dogs that have tasted blood
can never again be trusted
with sheep or lamb of God

Guttural blood thirsty gulls
gorged on fattened burgered flesh
gulls first choice now
over the wide world
seagulls scanned for well oiled skin
containing burger fried fat
converted into human flesh
that first spilled out on Falmouth pavements

The culling had begun
the war of worlds
of those above and those below
and who will win
the gods will know

Poem for Pinkies

Hello Pinkie — the night I found out

Are you going to Strawberry Fair
parsley sage raspberry and time
remember me -- the one who was there
mixing smoke with whisky and wine

He was sitting cross legged in a colourful tent
at the Strawberry Fair
— in a Cambridge summer
music entwining his words and spells
a teller of tales
his long dark ringlets
thin frame and sparking eyes intrigued me
we wrapped ourselves around the moment
and smiled across time — our time was now

Once upon a time outside the tent
he unfurled his enormous seven foot height
I asked him — seven foot two — wow
I said gazing up and smiled
this was magic
to have my very own giant in tow
I was as tall as his belt
my very own marsh-wiggle straight from the
Silver Chair
he was as tall as a tower
when we sat to eat on a friend's bench
his body was almost normal size
but his legs went on for ever

Tall and small we caused a visual stir
in the pubs as we trawled that summer scene
breathing in the festive airs of drifting laughter
summer's light echoed
on golden evening stonework
steeped in study

Hello Pinkie — I called to everyone we saw
as shadows darkened

Hello Pinkie — some called back
merrily marinated in grape — in hops
in hi high spirits

No one asked a question of the greeting
and I have no idea
And then ahead
a small Scot swaying in a kilt

I have to know — I ran ahead of my giant friend
I gently felled the Scot from behind
and reached up under his kilt
and grabbed his naked bum

It's true — I cried triumphant
it's true — we laughed
and sat on steps — sipping the malt whisky
he'd held high and saved from the felling
as Cambridge slowly spun around my head

And that was the night a giant carried me home

Sisterfield in Autumn

Mending broken bits of sisterness
that scatter the years with debris
which lie like wrecked car hulks
disappearing into mist

So many times we drove together
bent each others fender
crashed and left the battered wreckage
to litter the road
the only road we drive
our own private road to sister-field
at times we would be grabbing the wheel
from each other
then the screech of breaks

Perhaps we should have watched our speed
perhaps too often, we were driving in the dark

We do not want a bitter harvest
we have struggled to glean ripe corn
from our weed strewn field
we only have one field
which together we inherited
one field - that is ours alone to tend

Each time now we walk together
along the road towards our field
we have to be courageous
because we bring our bruised
and battered beings

to the task
scarred with bleeding feet
we tread with trepidation
our wounded hearts tremble
as we enter our field of weeds

Slowly from behind the cloud
above our field
sometimes the sun begins to shine
and warms us

Glimpsed in kaleidoscopic moments
the patterns are released
to freedoms flow
and colours sharp relief

We breathe the freshly scented air
and we become aware
our hearts no longer bleed

As we make plans to plough

Southwold Pier

Striding its sturdy columns defiantly out
into the — sometimes vicious — cold North Sea
It will not — we hope — set sail
taking a deep breath to walk its length
and down a coffee off we set
determined strides
to counter the bullying punching gusts

We are the winter warmer girls
coat wrapped — pull hatted
scarf knotted — winter booted
warm trousered — thermal vested
woollen socked — sturdy knickered
hands pocketed — gloves mislaid

As we stride out high winds and life elicit tears
and pound white waves beneath
the swirling sea is seen in spaces
through slightly shaking boardwalk planks
ruffling the pent up surging
that thunders underfoot

What was that you said — I said
oh never mind — what
words of wisdom lost and tossed
by wild uncaring gusts
our words are wind-whipped out of earshot
over the ice cold rail into a broiling sea
seated in a cold Tim Hunkin's metal booth
we get more swirling air

rugs and warming drinks tasting salt lips
hands shelter hot bitter shall I sugar it
coffee foam
hair whips into mouths as well as coffee
oh lets go inside
what

the clock-house back door slams
sheltered now we wonder now
about the possibility of cake
sweet mouthed we watch white horses thunder
there is no other show in town
I've got to go
and so must I
a chorus party piece of sugar speak
so
coat wrapping —pull hatting
scarf knotting — winter booting
warm trousering — thermal vesting
woollen stocking — sturdy knickers
deeply shocking
hand pocketed — gloves mislaid
door banging — determined striding
countering — gusting
bullying — punching
wild winds thrusting
while winter walking
on Southwold Pier

After Hafiz

My Heart is Glad — 4 am 28 March 2013

My heart is glad
I am tracking down wind of Hafiz
breathe in the aroma of sage on the wind
down wind — the Breath
is moving in the grasslands

Alchemised and conflagrated
the scents of the world
are offered up
in smokey sunlit trails
drifts through uncountable wildebeest
trailing through endless savannah
as incense drifting
through earthbound cities and temples
breathe in the aroma of sage on the wind

Breathe in
the scent of a day
the scent of a hundred years
the scent of an hour
the scent of starlight
take another deep-world breath
you are downwind of Rumi
down wind of Tao

Take a deep breath
breathe in the aroma of sage on the wind
feel the breeze that reminds us
where we are Beloved
that place is here and now
and is why my heart is glad

Dinosaurs Dancing

Théorie amusante

When gravity was lighter
before the meteor struck
dinosaurs could dance
light footed

The largest of them all
would dance on moonlit nights
amongst the giant nodding leaves
there were no flowers
was no grass

Centipedes yards long
tunnel through undergrowth
seeking pray

Dragonflies hover across the ponds
with drooping dripping fronds
shimmering on vast vibrating humming wings

Pterodactyls soar with ease
into balmy heat held skies
screaming skin tight light
on warm still lifts of air
lightly T-rex ambles
over swamp and rolling hillside
others — giant sprinters
speed amongst tall plants
and gently dripping horse-tail trees

All roam the earth both fast and wild
until it struck

As darkness rolled
earth's gravity became too heavy
to support their giant bones
as every giant plant collapsed
each dinosaur was grounded
floored into extinction
into the looming gloom
as we small things
begin our days

The Mosaic

A last day of school before Christmas
everyone is in the festive darkening hall
at six years old I think
it is down to the happiest one
I yell three cheers
when it is not my place to do so

Hip Hip …

A painful silence lengthens its long dark tale
poured on my heady exuberance
expectant of hooray

But the silence grows
into a monstrous shame filled shadow
as I fall into its darkening pit
and in that moment
it is broken
the beautiful vase
the vase that holds the flowering
of my six year old being
brim full of love
happiness – excitement
in that moment of public shame
the vase shatters into hundreds and
thousands of colourful pieces

Now I make mosaics of the broken bits instead

Exotic Garden – Four Poster

Layered sound sheets
distil and spill through unseen landscapes
lying beyond the tall tree curtains
the garden sprawl of a rumpled bed

The slow stretch of muscled torso trunk
wakes to light and ecstasy of summers warmth

A deeply distant voice
the drumbeat of a gate
are all outside the garden's leafy satin silks
which wrap around the dew dropped lawn
skeins of scattered sunlit threads
that draw the sweat of dawn

Emerging from shadowed night
long ebony fingers reach sensually across
the supine back
a lifting of light lawn lace –
now gradually revealed
is naked to the sky

As darkness unravels back
into crevice — bush caverns
are sensual invitation of sanctuary
to slowly retreating darkness

Sunlit tendrils of birdsong
are golden curls upon earths pillow
flowing from hidden places
as the garden lies
in supine morning glory
breathing in the rampant day

Persian Rug

Loom stretched
shuttle threaded
through sunlit laughter
a fabric map of life glows softly bright

In moonlight
mountains coldly wait
shouldering the wheel of stars
echoes pass from rock to rock
the deadly screeches of the night

All is woven into patterned life
shouts of men and boys
tears of wives and daughters
drop silently
darkening the spreading colours

Goats trembling cries stain the darkness
scents of smoke drift spices
into knotted threads
on a far flung courtyard terrace

A world away
now laid out
onto rich oak floor
colours slowly bleed
into sunlight
for a hundred years
They walk upon my back

The fluttering sounds that are their threads
drift down deep
into my pile
and are absorbed
as they too weave their days

The Phosphorescent Night

This was a night of nights
a night to imagine
a night to truly live
this night of wondrous real world magic
casting a spell
there is an escapade afoot

The two of us dressed
in velvet darkness
ascend the dunes

A dark panorama unfolds before us
far out to sea
distant cargos of light await the day

Sparkling strangely
the stars blink on and off
in low horizon
over the slowly stirring molasses sea

Whilst high above the beach
the star dome slowly wheels
its stately dance
in perfect step with time
and yet the lower sky
above the sea is host
to myriads of winking stars
we wonder at the magic cause of this

Searching for our treasured quest
we hear the suck and thrust of breathing waves
and see white starlit foam spit flow
from Neptune's mouth
we walk the sand bar shore
to find the phosphorescent sea
scanning dark water
for magical light waves
walking under a fisherman's line we wonder
maybe this is not the night

At last we see
a gently sparking wave of luminescence
an eerie light inside the rolling foam
and then another lighting up
the rolling tumble as it comes
restlessly reaching towards the shore
Now we see — we see the game
as all along the wave length is ignited
the dark sea surface further out
is all aglow now
the tarry water lit with sparkling sea stars
echoing the manifesting meteor shower above

The sea it seems
is lighting up for us
it seems to know our game and wants to play

We long to be enfolded in this magical event

Quickly naked we wade into the waves
each move we make

up-lights the waves
with strange cold fire
that is entrancing
we are dancing
we are the children
of an August night
magical beings
that can light up waves and water
as it swirls around us
as we play a symphony of sea and stars
we are reborn
gently immersed in a womb of dark water
infused with light

Baptised in this deluge of natural wonders
we are deeply surrendered to joy

We revel in the wonder and the sheer delight
of swimming in the phosphorescent night

Suffolk Summer

Along a Lane Near Halesworth

Time filters
sunlight down
the tranquil Suffolk lane

Tall oaks
in layered leafy summer skirts
like Spanish dancers twist
their bare arm boughs
thrown high towards
the dome of sky
reaching and recoiling
from half remembered toss
of dancing storms
now in still air
in gold leaf light
these tall grandees
these arbiters of time
stand sentinel
with time tracked shadows
and wrapped resplendent in dog rose cloaks
that overgrow the hedgerow in
exuberant summer frenzy
that is still still
still as if — through time — remains unchanged

The softest dog rose petal holds
the moment as
the summer lane unfolds
its summer dress and hugs
my naked shoulders in the sun

Southwold Sailors

Quotes are from historical records taken from The Sailors Reading Room, Southwold, Suffolk

Tossed in storms
they were
and biting east wind cold
screaming sometimes
as it tore into rope
loose oil skin and sail
gales buffeted their heaving bucking boats
strong faces turned
towards salt tearing blasts of Arctic air
the chilling dangers
of the vast dark churning waves

Better at reading clouds and stars
they had applied themselves to lettering
some more than others if truth be told
but Mrs Rayley had given them a place
of quietude and temperance
intoned on opening day - in terms they
understood

'A long pull
and a strong pull
and a pull together
securing benefit and hearts rejoicing'
Is what the reverend said

And so we shall lads — so we shall
a place to meet
and read the occurrences of the day
storms may rage out side
inside is quiet peace and safety
a place for sailors yarns
and visitors alike
a room set adrift a century and a half ago
the sea in which it bottle bobs
complete with replicated boats
held encased in moments
on the tide of time
fragments of men's lives are saved
for us to savour how they lived
to gather fish and hoist the sails
and head for home and shelter

Time-Beads

A bead the first
a seed
that scutters down
through dripping dappled leaves
and is received
by dark-rich pungent earth
to root and stem
that grow through air
carbonating spinning sunlight
into dancing green wands
that gift the air we breathe

Time-beads thread the turning earth
to warm-moon night and streaming sun

The slowly stretching tree
towers majestically through time
its rough bark host
to myriad insect worlds
and holds small claws that clutch to climb
to swing and fly
flowers spread out
from nectared sweet tongued depths
while dark-below buried droplets
sucked through root-ways
climb inside the vast trunk
to slake the thirst of leaves
and send breath skywards
making clouds

Another time-bead threads
as in the distance a new road growls
a road that brings the men with saws
that give the forest mange

A dark bead now is threaded

The chainsaw bites

During the long fall to earth
the vast tree groans
the men step back and stand
as if respectful of the fallen one

Another bead
In time

A world away
at a discrete distance
connection to its forest roots long severed
a new wood floor is laid
to rest
piece by piece
and money paid

Time-beads scatter across the sunlit floor
as children play the generations games

Finally there is a renovation
old boards ripped out
so pleasing to the speculators eye

More time-beads thread and tread
the beat of earth
and later still a fragment overheard
and half a world away
a man and child

There was a forest here
one time — I think

The long evening shadows
finger speculatively
the hard edge crack
of sun-warmed rocks
and reach towards the low-toned scream
of empty sand and sky

St Peter, St Paul and all the Angels of Wangford

Angels of wood Angels of glass
Angels of stone Angels of brass

Invisible angels glide
floating on mist above the Priory Marsh
the church raises its gargoyled tower
ancient monastic roots coiled in time
reach now into the quarter hour chime

High above the reverential heads
the hymning valence draw of generations
to this place where angels spread
their vibrant wings halfway to heaven
flocked in ancient timbers
shouldering the roof

Some winged ones pray
some bring crowned gifts of gold
and some harp music and the drum
some simply observe
the ways of human kind below

Tis said that angels honour
the dappled dark and light
of worldly life and times

A host of four score angels grace
this beautiful and holy place
where angel dust has fallen
down the sweep of years
in their calm presence stills

As darkness clears the apex of the roof
see angel faces shelter there aloof
the remnants of the Cluniac past
they are the Ancient ones — the last

Come — be dizzied
by joyous angels flying round
They have forever graced
this angeled ground

Black Dog

A Suffolk Legend of Beccles, Blythburgh and Dunwich

Hell had opened its gaping mouth
black storm coated the sky
hairs rose on man and dog alike
the air had trembled
in the heat of that long afternoon

Suddenly a fireball cracked a deafening roar
that broke the steeple
stopping time itself
broke time in pieces hands and all

Hail drove harsh ice knives
into smoking thatch and steeple
into flesh

People ran from that sky-born hound of hell
ran from screaming streaming eye of storm
into the sanctified house
and prayed
prayed for deliverance
and tried to sing a punctuated hymn
but — has to be said — they were all sinners

Lightening blazed
                        and spat its light
                    onto the villagers cowering heads
                    then the great door blew agape
        the growling maelstrom came marauding
into church
with the roaring wind and rain
caught in the spotlight one great howl
and then another – human howl
a body dragged into the aisle
a throat torn open
blood and flesh and rolling eyes
a scream of pain
                  and then again

A wrenching of hearts
              a tearing of flesh
                  a torment of sky
                      the howling scream of wind
                          commingled cries of fear

The stench of a great wet dog
                the iron smell of pooling dripping blood
                          and then the dog was gone

The devil ran 12 miles
              with dripping mouth and paws and claws
                        and bloodied coat

With raging breath it clawed and burned
the great closed doors of Blythburgh church
then turned away
the great brute
killed and maimed
the ale wives drunken men
who had not got to church
so they were burned by the devilled breath
that made a Suffolk legend

Full on to Dunwich streets t'ward dawn
an' tossed a rat fer measure
some say there was a babee gone
a chile that's lost forever

It was a Devil Dog fer sure
they say it sailed away from shore
last seen aboard a Flanders bound
that Devil beast
that bloodied hound
an' never more its like was found

It left a tale fer us to tell
Of bloodied Black Shuk
                    dog from hell

Dripping With Butter and Marmite

Steaming from the Aga
clutched in huge round toasters
I delight in the taste
of winter crumpets
dripping with butter and marmite

Memories of splashing
my winter welly boots
into petrol rainbowed puddles
as I battle home from school
through darkening skies
of storm tossed birds and leaves

Beret and Mackintosh
buttoned and belted
leaning against the damp west wind
my small feet are sturdily laced
(a new learned skill)
into shiny new clodhoppers
with room to grow into

Every bit of me
has room to grow into
is bursting to grow into
the me that isn't yet

Snowdrops

In a Wood above Dunwich Beach

After Wordsworth's Daffodils

I wandered lonely as the sea
that floats white foam upon its tide
when all at once what did I see
a host of snowdrops far and wide
beside the sea beneath the trees
white heads dipping in the breeze

And scattered as the starlight shines
and twinkles in the milky way,
they stretch in ever-winding rhymes
all through the woods above the bay
Ten thousand saw them at a glance
spread through the wood in gentle dance

the waves below them danced but they
out-did the sparkling waves for me
a poet hears pans music play
whilst in such a fragile company
I gazed and gazed but little thought
of wealth the sight to me had brought

For now when on my bed I lie
in meditative thoughtful mood
they flash into that inward eye
that knows the bliss of solitude

And then my heart with pleasure could
be dancing in that snow drop wood

And then my heart with pleasure will
be dancing with those snowdrops still

Stillwater

Meditation with a drop of water

The drop that you hold in your hand
is part of the water which was the cradle of all life
on this planet aeons ago
the first rain that splashed down on the hot earth
to form the first sea.
each drop, in sunlight
has risen from the sea in countless ages
and fallen to the earth again
as rain

The drop that you hold in your hand
has been a prism forming myriad rainbows
has travelled underground streams
bubbling through dark caverns
the architect of cathedral caves
formed valleys
and split granite

The drop that you hold in your hand
has flowed down broad rivers
has risen in the sap of trees
has been the sweat of slaves
and the tears of children
it has become the foam topped waves
and deep unfathomable depths
of vast dark lakes
and seas

The drop that you hold in your hand
has been part of the great flood
it has been a dewdrop on a blade of grass
a drop that has pounded
through the hearts of whales in blood
and lain in an eagle's egg
it has travelled in the fluid of a poet's brain
and dripped from the wounds of the dying

The drop that you hold in your hand
has been trapped in the snows of the arctic
reflected the sun in a desert oasis
and refreshed the weary

This drop
unimaginably old
yet fresh and new
is evaporating slowly from your hand
to mingle with the air you breathe, perhaps
or drift in a sun-topped cloud
a thousand feet above the earth

Imagine its journey from your hand
where will it go?
you can direct its journey
as it evaporates
send your consciousness with it
It is the water of life
It is still water

Harvest Home

Cradling a tin of peas
against my coat
I am three years old
holding it in wonder
a cupboard-shelf thing in my arms
strangely it sloshes inside

The tree high man stands by the church door
I do not hold my mothers hand
the baby's shawl froths down towards me
importantly I hold the tin and find our pew

The church is full of colour
unfamiliar shapes and smells
a great sheaf loaf shines in leaded window light
my footsteps are new to me in shining shoes
as I tread on deep organ notes
over strangely exciting floor grills
and writing stones
towards the box of unfamiliar packets
filled with a word I have only just heard—
'produce'

The grow-nups sing a hymn about fields
I look up at the Jesus man bleeding
His body shines like the man in the field
when I saw the great red harvester
churning out the tight string bales
for us to sit on

The harvest tea is noisy and shiny
it comes with ladies
with flowers on their pinnies
and hard shampoo-n-set hair
they give me horrid orange squash
I ask for tea — Mummy gives me tea I tell them
Mummy's on the big people's table
I am with funny smelling village children
I do not know — my legs swing under the table
the food does not taste like home
I drop some under the table and feel worried
they will know its my sandwich — my cake

When we are allowed
I get down and find Mummy
I don't like harvest
I want to go home

Time

Written when I was nine years old

The mists of time move steadily
hour after hour — day by day
yet century by century
never heading on its way

The clouds of time go on and on
on on on
nothing stops them
time is neither short nor long
no human knows from whence it came

The past is measured in time
though we don't know how much
time — time — it weakens or strengthens
our limbs
But time is such

Time gives love and time gives hate
time gives us time to learn
time gives us fortune or Fate
but time the past does burn

It makes the future come alive
and then it is the past
time makes our babes arrive
and gives us peace at last

Zanzibar Women

They drifted through the late afternoon shallows
their gentle laughters' chatter
lapping at the shore
a gathering of wading women
weaving their voices together
from beyond a further shore
we wondered what they gathered for

As they neared we saw the purpose
in their near shore drift
through blood warm tranquil turquoise
of limpid libation to Zanzibar gods

Many were pulling a long net behind
through knee high water
they made it seem an easy task
to walk with babies and the net
others further out and nearer laughed
calling out with gentle splashes
herding
the small shoals gather in the swirl
turning
the women become encirclers
drawing toward each other and the shore

We could see their small sea silver jewels
leaping to be free now
as the water shallowed to the sand

Before their flashings had been lulling
in the drifting women's wake
urgent now small fry became aware
of dangers in the dance of time

Soon on shore
there was one heap of tiny twitching treasure
destined for the pots and pails
that magically appear
from heads and folds of brightly coloured clothes

A pile silver treasure apportioned and discussed
and thus divided into smaller piles
some for each to take away
for family at end of day

No blood-lust hunt — just women fun
an afternoon adrift in sun
and gentleness of harvest
was those women's way
together they had fed — with small fry
all their Zanzibar village
by the end of the gathering day

Altar'ed States

Fool's Night

Dusty canticles were sung
filtering the sparkling motes of dust
bathing the high and arching space
in deeply noted soul surge song
From punctuated cells they had spilled out
gliding in cloisters through shadowed archways
in evensong light – last light of day

One face looked up onto the light
all others being cowled and bowed
looked up with longing
from his past as tumbler fool and juggler once
to kings and gentle folk and market place
it was his love to entertain the crowd
yet now it was so often that his head was bowed
in simple act of bringing life to spidered text
just in the margin he would humbly brush
bright colour that would make the pages dance

My God is love and I do love my God
and I would love to entertain my Lord
and so I will before the Sadness of His Cross

So deep in light of moon he tiptoes from his cell
his old fool horn-ed cap
with one long silenced but remembered bell
is in his pack with parti coloured boots

In reverential dark he changes into light
juggles and tumbles
into the vaulted vastness of that sacred space
his greatest gift is given deep into the night
With audience of saints
which branching shadows lace
and yet none save one
small angel smiles
as one old hidden abbot sees the show

One that told the tale and passed it on
in vespered whispers down the years
so still — into our time
it reaches into modern ears
tumbling down a thousand years

The First One

Imagine – heading out
to sea – to see no compass
                                        just heading
                                        heading away
From land
into waters no-one has charted
crossing the link-water
to find another land
perhaps
or drop off the edge
                                        of the world
with raft — with sail — with paddle

Plunge

Into wave-water
    into wind-sky

I'll go to the edge and then come back
just to see what's beyond the beyond
where we don't know
                    where we can't see

You may not be able to return
sea could take you
down in her swirl skirt

I'll take the risk – I have to try

Why – why – why

Sea the seabird high in the sun-drift
and know my eyes and soul are drawn
towards the edges of worlds
I have to grow
I have to go
it draws me out to sea

And now we fly — on and on
drifting into the blue
a lost plane flies through night and day
fears of falling with screaming engines
into the swallowing sea
at last to dive dissolve
into the coldest deep

With all our modern waves
we cannot find them
as they drift drown and down
into the dark of unknowing

Ideas of Flight

Duologue – a Fragment

I can teach you
there's a clearing in the wood

You'll see it's an exciting feeling
to fly above the tree tops
the wind in your hair
to soar with the birds
I almost collided with a bat the other night
what a shocker

No not yet
just a few others – and you
it's an ability we lost
I don't know when or how

It's a special mind body co-ordination
here we are – I flew round here the other nite
I'll show you how its done
then you can try
arms low and slightly back
head up and think yourself into lift off
palms flat and push behind you
knowing you can do it
as you push palms back
chest out – onto toes
that's right
your nearly there
you almost lifted off that time

I'll show you — see
it's such a great feeling see — wheee
up and round and swooping
and gently landing
now you try — just try —oops
now get ready
feel the possibility of lift off in your bones
lift — lift — lift

Don't try too hard
just feel an 'I can do it' confidence
push back with your palms — chest out
head up –lift onto your toes
leave the ground behind
you're almost — almost — almost — yes

There you go
I knew you could do it

Soon I'm going to teach the whole world to fly

The Queen

The view from here

Often I wave in my sleep
I see the faces slowly passing
waving back
with their little flags
I sometimes wonder about their lives
in their small
row after row houses
no corridors to roam about in
no staff
I wonder what its like
to do the washing up
or actually make a cup of tea

Sometimes I feed the corgis
just for fun
I tell the horses things
no-one else can hear
it's fun when they snort
in agreement

So many state occasions
so many things to open
so many people to meet
sometimes I tire of it
and want to
shall I tell
it was Marylyn's idea
she would walk about unrecognised

Do you want to see Marylyn
she asked her friend
as they walked on the street

She shook out her hair from her scarf
retied the belt of her rain coat
sashayed along the pavement
and became her screen self
as people started exclaiming and pointing

That's when we got the idea
to slip out of the royal garden
and get on a bus
the passages were empty
in the dark kitchen the corgis stirred
but did not wake
they are well fed

Carefully slipping the backdoor bolt
I found an old coat in a shed
close to the wall
there was a door in the wall
by a compost heap

The late night streets were neon bright
rowdy with noise
but one stood ones ground
and waited for an actual bus

One had to get off at the next stop
one had forgotten one needs money
out there

Caroline Dirty Green

Caroline Dirty Green considers cheap washing-
up liquid
instead of the one that doesn't kill fish

Caroline Clean Green always picks up the green
option
in the sure knowledge that it will keep her green
clean as well as fashionably impoverished

Dirty mucky Green (Caroline) will consider
buying something that isn't ethically sourced
but has much brighter packaging

Clean Caroline Green will remain
completely calm
choosing only the fair trade option
that doesn't involve small children in the process
being held prisoner by horrid people

Caroline Dirty Green will buy quite a lot of
clothes
from shops that sell things
made by manufacturers
that exploit their work force in hot countries
far away from the High Street

Caroline Clean Green is completely consumer free
and will only buy what she needs from charity shops
make it herself from fair traded materials
and sleep well at night

Caroline Dirty Green leaves lighting and heating on
when the house is empty because she cant be bothered to check
and it doesn't matter anyway

Caroline Clean Green will always check
before she goes out
and never leave an empty room
without switching off all lights and standbys

Somewhere between the two of us
is Caroline Mid Green
who does all of the above sometimes
but is getting gradually greener
but sometimes just can't not buy that saucy pair of red shoes
that are completely irresistible
and can get her into all sorts of unethically saucy trouble
which she thoroughly enjoys

Caroline Large and Caroline Small

Caroline Large raises money for charity
and has even given her last sandwich to a street beggar
Caroline Small walks past
pretending not to notice

Caroline Large can fire-walk
Caroline Small cannot stand on an underground platform
and has to lurk in the passageway

Caroline Large (who's not afraid of anything)
went on the London Eye on a beautiful sunny day
Caroline Small kept her eyes shut all the way round.

Caroline Small couldn't fly for 15 years
after getting a panic attack
Caroline Large has flown half way around the world

Caroline Large can get a standing ovation.
Caroline Small couldn't

Caroline Large is the mum of a secret millionaire
Caroline Small pays for groceries with small change
she keeps in a jar on the shelf

Caroline Large turns heads
as she walks into the newest trendy bar in town
No one notices Caroline Small
on the bus carrying her shopping bag

Fables

Hopelessness is worse on sunny days
if weather matches mood
there is a quantum solace
a sanctuary of soul
within the endless trudging despair
of days unsought

And so she thought
that flying down
the savage falling scream
of life tearing from living body
into the deep ravine
the smash of flesh on rock
bloodying the churning water
extinguishing a life in darkness
would be release

But then he passed her
whispered — find a seed

Middle Earth

And just around the corner
there is our hobbit meeting house
where we sit in silence with our thoughts
or no thoughts
deep we go
deeper than the roots of mountains
or lighter than briar smoke
which is particularly attracted
to starlight and clouds
it is a special place
and so's this path
protected by tangled magic
woven by elves in times long ago
see
the colour comes as we walk along
brightening our way

The Drop

A dewdrop on a blade of grass
  pausing
    water-falling
      tracing on leaves
        the memory of stars

An image of the sun
  roles within its slow
                  decent
dropping earthward
  slowly softening into soil
before its journey skywards
      breathing into clouds

It is a shining traveler
through both time and space
so present at its birth
  brings life to life on earth

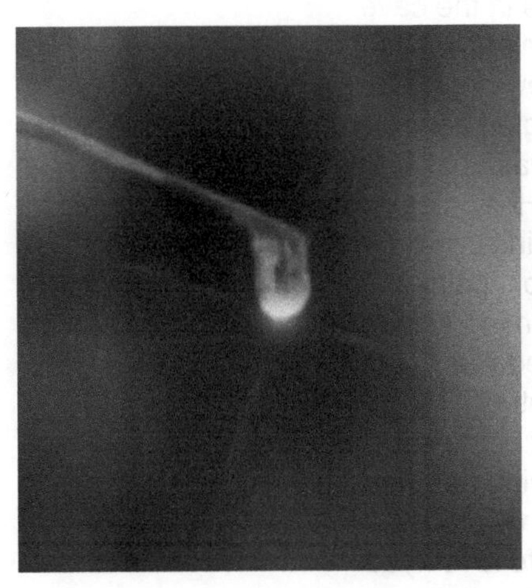

Earth Diva

Image of the Goddess I

She was in the cave
when She saw him
She knew he would subdue
Her tangled abundance
shock waves of sadness
rocked Her
ricocheting down the ages
intolerable pain
of screaming whales and trees
splintered Her heart
fragmented
Her hurt being sought refuge
in the living darknesses
the eternal places
where life is relayed
passed from past
to future

And he was coming
there was no doubt
no falter in his stride
he was hunting Her herds
he embodied hordes
from the untameable
he would draw blood
he would protect
everything that bowed to his will
in his stride
and in his power
a different kind of darkness
pervades
his stockades

As they emerged together
from their dark places
with light energy
dancing over and through
and step with step
they understand
that new strengths flow
from this new land

Rainforest Diva

Image of the Goddess II

Green She towered
great Her power
fecundity Her theme
She is cloud maker
kaleidoscope colours cascade
and kindled to fast fruition
stately exotic paradisian
She reigns in the forest

Her tree was falling in a screaming arc
an arching aching cry
of proud yet pleading desperation
before the death drum thud
thundered its reverberation.
they soiled her soil
these chain males
with their growling chain saws
bit savagely into Her vulnerability
hot fever raged and burned
fires festered and grew
strangely silent
She lifted Her scarred face
towards the sun
as clouds of smoke
obscured vision

The smoke signals were seen
in places far from earth
by satellites
financiers and socialites
those who never scratched the soil
or cut a tree
felt some small culpability
felt sense of loss
that now impinged
on their tight packaged lives
and though removed
the forest rain
commingled tears
as smoke got in their eyes

Sea Diva

Image of the Goddess III

Soft light on tranquil shore
the night heralds afar off
golden salamanders play in sunset waves
gradually they drown
and only sea gulls cry
their lost lament
at cliff hard rocks
that sometimes break
with irreparable finality
into the sea that takes

She takes filth into Her bed
She has become a whore
what man ejects into Her waves
She accepts
and still
looks beautiful — in a good light
whatever the polluting aspect of his actions
he expects Her to take it
he knows She will take it
and hide his excess
occasional seal cubs found floating
symbolically denote a deeper dirt disease

And yet in past millennia
She embodied purity
when the spirit moved upon Her
She gave birth exuberantly
in reverence Sea was
the first immaculate conception
this virgin birth spawned mankind
who uses her without restraint
so far from adoration
he practises abuse of Her creation
and in his panting haste
he fills Her with his waste
and flies blue flags proclaiming all is well
so time will tell

But is it hell

Doggerland

Speculate
upon a long lost land
a kingdom there was — perhaps
but now without a king
or kitchen maid

From long lost lands
some dripping bones are dredged
deck dried
upon the cold sea swell
the fisherfolk have tales to tell
We see
the look
of this lost land
its long drowned worlds
build pictures
of an ancient people
living out their days

Animals there were to tend
meadows - wind blown
nodding flower heads and corn
they heard the birds call out with each new dawn

Sea raised a water wall
which drowned a people
overwhelmed a way of life

Oh ancient Dogger people
    your long lost lands
                    now fathoms deep in time
                    marinated in the brine
high seas rising — rising
breaking over heads
as waves sweep in and swallow
                    sending souls
                    swirling deeply under shoals
below the rocking waves
where cradled children sleep
slowly silting into drowning sands
that once were rolling lands
of these forgotten people
their dripping bones
dredged now
and torn
from ancient sandy beds of rest
no voices left to cry
do not disturb
are left to dry

Speculate
our own long drowned demise in some far
or not so far-off futured scene
with dark waves rolling deep above
our long lost land
a thought is played
of what there might have been
a kingdom here — perhaps
with king and kitchen maid
It may be so — the way it was begins to fade

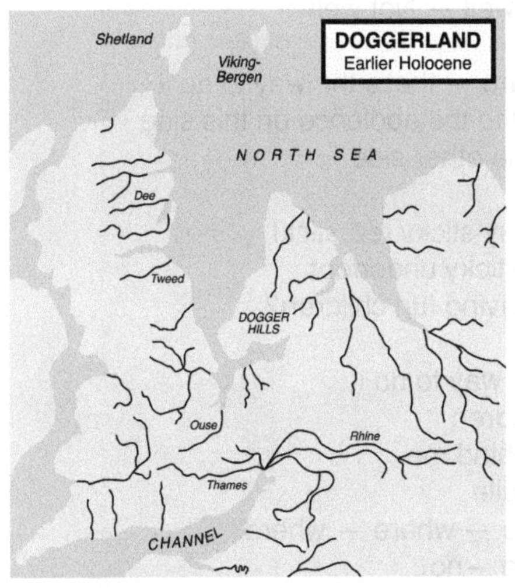

Map showing hypothetical extent of Doggerland (c. 8,000 BC), which provided a land bridge between Britain and the Continent

Punch Box

That's the way to do it
Judy – Judy – Judy
not mad not mad not
Am am am
Well well well – Not well

Wham slam – that's the way to do it
and I bow to the audience on this side
then on the other side

Where's my sticky red stick!
sticky – sticky underfoot
are you having fun children?

That's the way to do it
isn't it children
whose behind me
the crocodile
behind me – where – where
I look here –no
and here – no no no
naughty children
there's no one behind me
oh no there isn't
is
isn't

Ow
It bit me
naughty naughty crocodile
where's my big sticky stick
bang bang bang — that's the way to do it
let's get more sausages
out you go with your bitey teeth
eat the sausages — eat the lot
oh dearie, dearie me
Judy — Judy — Judy mincing mincing Judy
Mrs Punch is sausages
Mrs Punch is sausages
who said that

Was not — Was not
was not me ! was was

I didn't — didn't — did
oh dearie dearie me — I am in a muddle
dee dah dee dah that's the way to do it
Mr Plod is knocking on at the door
run run run
shredded into scattered pieces
screaming into darkness
torn from mum – mum!
tearing the homespun fabric of torn tears
overflowing frightened eyes

Darkness

No Dad no
into the dark earth potato sack
potatoes emptied into a car boot
kicking out-trying to escape
trying to reach her
back through darkness – Mum

Threatened into silence
by stunning blows
a small boy cowers
in the bottom of a sack
smelling earth then urine
as trousers flood with warmth
waking later ears ringing

Feeling angry at mum
for being weak
for making Dad angry
for hearing searing condemnation
of her easy ways
it's her fault Dad needs a drink
her fault he's in this stinking sack
he wakes again shivering
silence — Dad —Dad
no reply

On the road occasionally fed
treated like a dog
Dad cushions his head
in mockery of love that stifles breath
a bear hug squeeze - a vice of fierce hugging
distorting a small boys rib cage
changing the shape and growth of his heart

Years later
And too late
dumped on mothers doorstep

He despises his brothers' softly quiet ways

Brain box – brain your box
box your ears and take the jeers
I know your fears
I know your fears that make your tears
be a man now if you can
you hide your hide
your hide I'll tan

Until the silt builds up
dark layer on layer
of dark thoughts
knocking at the door
having hurt and hurting he walks away

Weeks of coastal drifting
one day into the next
one sun filled day
he finds the shadow on the sand
of a small stripy castle
encircled by children watching
the dark king of the stripy shack

Draw the children
Into your world professor
Punch Punch Punch
knock'm dead
until they bled
until they bled
and stain the sand with laughter

That's the way to do it
bash the baby
bash Mrs Punch
she's only a puppet
made to be bashed
ooh! the baby is crying
and it must must must be stopped
bang bash bash
thats the way to do it

Tick-tock — quiet children
there is always the crocodile
with toothy grim grin
a black hole space sucker
leaps out to grab the darkness inside
land seeps into marshland
sucking its struggling victims dark dark down
blowing out the willow wisp
then into darkness into go…

Potato head
they shout
at the hunched hood
towards unseeing dulled down eyes
a playground puppet

Glasses darken
glasses darken eyes in pain
from glaring cauterising sun
as he's twisted tightly
turning into a glaring son
a son so small - so very small
looming a large shadow into the weave
over the shaking shivering creature
deeply embedded like a festering thorn

Whisky yelling breath and gin for quieting
daren't breathe
daren't breathe

A hungry boy sits watching on the sand
watching the stripy tent set up
watching the hiding man Mr Punch
inside his theatre box
always hunch back
always smiling a leering smile
Always innocent of crimes
they see it all — the little children
violent grooming stickily absorbed
like sherbet on the tongue
clever clever clever
that's the way to do it
bash bash bash
that's the way to do it
oh no I didn't
didn't did 'didn't
confusing little minds
hello boys — and girls

One day he's all grown up
a dark young man –
all grown up — but twisted inside
Into small scrumpled pieces

The sand professor knows him
has taken him into his world
has felt him over time
there is penetration
hot breath – familiar pain in the shadows
of the small striped tent

One night the moon drifts
over a cooling body
staining sand

Next day the punch box is far away
a stopped clock propped-
proclaims performance at two

The strange strained voice is in his mouth
the strange stained voice is in his head

And on a beach a man is dead
and in a heart no feeling

My Grandfather Poem

The deafening explosion rips
through time and place
scattering shrapnel
throughout our family harvest
a century of life in flesh and bone
of bread and blood spilled wine
shattered in passed down broken pain

Ordinance
damaged my unknown grandfather
grotesqued in pain and twisted brain
outbursts of rage prowled and pounced
through damaged years

Shrapnel still
still leaves my son shaking in darkness
unable to outdistance fear

Even now we feel the absence of the fallen
disintegrated early into golem mud
their lack is still gut wrenching
our world out of shape

As we now stumble tumble screaming
into extended worlds of pain
deafening explosion
scatters shrapnel still
grips flesh and bone
with hurt passed down

Deafening explosion
damages my unknown grandfather
shrapnel still leaves sons and daughters
in shaking darkness
unable to outdistance fear

Even now we feel the absence of the fallen
disintegrated early into desert dust
or swollen tides
their lack is still gut wrenching
our world out of shape
as we now stumble
into other worlds of pain
into other deafness

Mute in silence do we stand and mourn
our own depleted harvest

The Xanadu Chronicles

Xana – song of songs

Entering the pleasure dome I danced with the
soaring space of it
I danced with the light
with the winds blowing in the long long curtains
that drew me out onto the great balcony
to see the lands stretching below me
to rise up to the high mountains
the scent of the flowers from the gardens
filled my breath with joy
to be here
inside the vast pleasure dome
the one I had seen from my bed loft
in the foot hills
to be here in fullness of sensual delight
my heart and soul leaping into the vaulted space
where I am whirling and whirling
around and around
and then to fall on soft cushions
to love and be loved
to remember his arms
to still feel his kisses on my swollen lips
to remember the night of nights
to sleep only as the birds begin
to sing in the willows

As evening falls the stately procession of dishes
mingled aromas to delight the senses
leopards slouching in on silver chains
the silver players from India
the clash of cymbals
the great gong master — a giant of a man
pounding his shimmering deep throated gongs
all were feasts for the eyes and senses

I knew now that I was born to dance
under the pleasure dome of vast expanse
the cedar-wood boxes of pleas
were once a year bought to the Khan
each box contained a parchment role
each one sealed with wax and silk ribbon
each one to be brought by a beautiful dancer
who would dance her plea
with eyes and her hands
and lithe bejewelled body
nine pleas were chosen with the rest consigned
to conflagration and lamentation

Once long ago in the mists of time
it was said there was a girl child who danced
she was very small with beautiful green eyes
as she emerged from the curtains
with one great leap
and danced with exquisite movement
the Khan's court gasped in wonder and surprise

At the Khan's feet she opened her box
and unrolled her small rolled plea
The Great Khan raised his hand

The nine have been chosen – you are too late
you are too young to dance The Dance of Pleas

Sadly she bowed her head
onto her small cedar box
she had found a gate
that led into the Khan's garden
she did not know
there were rules about dancing
raising her head
with two shining tears on her cheeks
she looked directly into the Khan's deep eyes
and simply said 'I did not know'
and started to tremble

A wise man who stood beside the Khan
whispered in his ear
'I will accept the child's plea'
intoned the smiling Khan
'from now on I will accept
a child's plea every year
we shall have the nine plus one
a minor's plea
and that will make infinity

From now on all children in my kingdom
will be allowed some time to play
it is my pleasure to watch

you dance now little one
It will be my pleasure to watch my children play
from Xanadu to the borders of Babylon
all children in our kingdom will have time to play'

In Xanadu in rose twilight
the golden pleasure dome would glow
dark flocks of birds would stir the sky
and people all would climb up high
to seek the guidance of their flow
like magic smoke they'd ring the tower
and herald darkness for an hour
until the lode star pierced the night
as people hummed with sheer delight
and gentle mandolins would strum
on rooftops and in gardens hung

The sages say light rain of stars
doth bring good fortune to the hearth

And those that hear the stars of night
dance all their lives with sheer delight

Each night as stardust drifted down
on dreaming hills and in the town
in reverential hands t'was kept
on land and sea while people slept
they gathered up the dust of stars
in special rounded shining jars

Fragment

They don't want to go any more
yes I heard it too
far less are taking the plunge to earth
they just don't want to be born there
oh yes normal amounts of males
but females its understandable
many who begin life there
are killed before first breath
because of gender

And so many are raped — murdered
mutilated — kept as house slaves
In fact I heard the other day
that it was almost impossible for them
to get through a life
without violation of some kind
simply because they chose that gender

No I wouldn't go
I think the ones who do are brave
it's too much a man's world down there
far too gender based
let them get on with it I say

Then of course the species will die out
but no bad thing
they had their chance
me — I'm scheduled for another world
multi-gendered
where they all eat plants

Eartha

Beautiful in lights and darks of sun and moon
she spins around dancing the dance
of space and time
those who see the deep of beauty of her being
draw in breath
in awe of the natural presence of her wilds

Now sold as slave to man
she falters
her beautiful body repeatedly raped
is unable to rest
her life force begins to fracture
her long rain forest hair is lost to mange
Eartha's man mined sores have became
infected

She has become choked
and short of breath in Jakarta
cold has gripped her heart in America
Atlantic sweat pours from her feverish body
her wet sheets are spread across our island
but we feel
there is little we could do
her man child is terminally addicted to his vices
he will not see his dying mother
or admit she is dying at all

But somewhere buried deeply
in his soul he may feel a certain lack

But parties all the harder
to drown the growing silence out

As Eartha drifts
uneasily through nights and days
lost in delirium

The Churchyard

When we came
there were long whispering grasses
a tangled abundance of habitat and mystery
a view of peaceful ages past
layers of time and place
had settled down the years
trees with long tendrils graced our view
the softly verdant lace of nature
covered and clothed the old stone markers

With harsh machines
that broke our hearts and windows
the old grey flesh of stones
now lie naked to the sky
like old and broken teeth they gape exposed
and joyless amongst the close shorn grass
our view destroyed as we look out
we make our eyes unseeing
of the cuts and thrusts
of such sad soulless tidiness

Inmates of Faith

On our planet
some walk
carrying dark prisons
around with them
peering through slots
in the dark
that surrounds them

Inmates of faith
they may or may not
smile into the fabric of shadows
knowing their lips
are never seen

Inmates of faith
may or may not
silently whisper
into darkness
knowing their lips
will never be seen
by the outer world

In our world
there are others
who are allowed to show
only their faces
the rest is wrapped
in the whispering weave
of faiths fabric

In our world
one of them has spoken out
has asked for education
has been shot
is fighting for life
that painful bullet is now lodged
in every covered head

Wedding of Hermione and Serhan

Banks of the Bosphorus — 19 July 2014

A plethora of pathways led you
to The Place of Now
this place where you now stand
in love together
before this company of friends and family

Marriage is the promise of a lifetime
- within its gold encircled ring of love
- is a ring of fire
- that forges a friendship that deepens
- an understanding that ripens
- a commitment to be with one another
- that transcends time and space

Ultimately it is an exploration
into the fabric of life itself
to journey together
through the highways and byways of life

Together you create a unique bond of love
delicate — light — yet fiercely strong filaments
known only to yourselves
let the hot light of this day
forever light your way
let your promises be kept
wildly – wonderfully and well!

Let the smile of love in your hearts
be spread like fabulous seeds of joy
today and every day
for the rest of your life together

Sometimes there may be brokenness
but remember whatever breaks
can be mended with gold
- it is a blessing
- that is kintsugi
- let your gold ring
remind you — each day — of your love
as the gold of the sun
reaches through space it touches
gold to gold
the alchemy of love
is your hearts' gold

Poet Mum

Characters 1/2/3

1 / What do you want us to eat?

2/ I'm writing a poem

1/ Shall we eat the fish you got tonight?

2/ I'm just getting a line finished

3/ (from other room) Mum we need to talk –
Now!

2/ I've just got to finish this for tonight

1/ So what shall we have tonight?

2/ Can't think- you decide

3/ (from other room) Mum!

2/ Aah - just give me a minute – I don't really
want to eat before class

3/ But mum we must talk before you go- cos i
have to know now

2/ I just want to finish this line and print it
Please!

1/ Where did that come from? Why are you screaming?

3/ Whats wrong Mum?

2/ Aaah!

The Dandelion Clock and the Air Hostess

Blown from your own air
just now taken in

the air bridge you have walked through life
with waves of air
myriads of countless times
breath blown

the feathered seeds drift out
dispersed to pitch and toss
upon the floating air

the deep'ning
of the unknown breath you take
to make a map of minutes

you breathe your way
through sobs and smiles
and sunlit moments
in your ark of life

fine stitches of the in and out of breath
that sews the fabric of our constant now

until you're out of breath and out of time

Leaking Moonlight at 11

Stars with moonlight leak romance
into the darkening landscape

as nightjars spread their shadowed sound
across the wood-lined fields
across the Autumn furrows

Bill and I stumble towards
the muffled hay barn
where we kiss when we arrive
to twine and writhe our bodies
long to lie platted
into hay's sweet warmth and smell

while stars and moonlight leak romance
onto our young limbs
shadowed into darkening landscape

Vampire General

Many medals shone
from on his chest
for bravery in blood campaigns

living across time
the Vampire General
influenced outcomes
sowed distrust
after battle

deep in the night
he called them all to feast
on those still groaning
for release
who would become the willing victims
choosing to be undead
swelling the vampire hoards
rising from their killing fields
to caverns to await the night

He was there at the signing
at the writing of the scroll
to enshrine the right to bear arms
and thus ensured that blood was spilt
in gangland and domestic wars

Each day in perpetuity
drawn to US soil
nightly they swarm
over the landscape of the dead
with supernatural skill
they smell the living stench
and suck their tender wounds
blood warm

spit bullets out like pips
gathering new souls
unto their Vampire swarm

Gingham Bale

The very first day
of big school sewing
beige skirt bottomed
she threw wide
the cupboard dresser draws
colour flooded through
the darkness of the day
the unfamiliar smell
of dressed cloth
the excitement of new material
for our work

asked to put our hands up
as she called a colour
my eyes were drawn
to the lowest bale
the black

Black Gingham

I thought gingham
meant bright coloured squares with white
but here was a revelation
black gingham
for my self-made plimsol bag
for black daps
perfectly matched

the others chose the colour

I felt excitement swelling
with my black gingham bale
the only one
who had a bale alone
soon to be cut and sewn

Interesting — perhaps
'witch' colour I chose
and what I now keep of spells
in my old black gingham bag
which now in time is almost rag

Dyslexic Witch

As a child I always got
my spelling wrong

Now I know my spells
were mirror bright

I have been left in their world
alone
without the others
that I see
in glimpses
on the edge of vision

Now I have learnt
mostly to disguise
the strangeness of my ways

and mostly I have learned
their spells correctly

but there has been a cost
and something has been lost